HEINEMANN FRONTLINE SERIES
The Eye of the Earth
Niyi Osundare

Niyi Osundare, born in 1947 at Ikere-Ekiti in Ondo State, had his secondary education at Amoye Grammar School, Ikere-Ekiti and Christ's School, Ado-Ekiti. He later went to the University of Ibadan where he graduated with a B.A. honours degree in English in 1972. He had his M.A. from Leeds University in 1974, and the Ph.D in 1979 from York University, Toronto.

Currently a Senior Lecturer in English at the University of Ibadan, Osundare who teaches Creative Writing, Stylistics, Sociology of Language and Literature and African Literature, is also a critic and a well-known poet in Nigeria. He is a columnist for *Newswatch* magazine.

Niyi Osundare is published in various local and international journals and magazines. His published volumes of poetry include *Songs of the Marketplace* (1983), *Village Voices* (1984), and *A Nib in the Pond* (1986). His poem, "It's the Harmattan", won the first prize in the 1968 Western State Festival of Arts and Culture. It also won one of the principal book prizes in the 1981 BBC 'Arts and Africa' Award. His second collection, *Village Voices* got an honourable mention in the 1986 Noma Award for publishing in Africa while *The Eye of the Earth* won both the 1986 Association of Nigerian Authors (ANA) prize for poetry and the 1986 Commonwealth poetry prize.

His current poetry column, "Songs of the Season", in the *Sunday Tribune* will be published in the Heinemann Frontline Series (*Frontliners*).

OTHER HEINEMANN FRONTLINERS

Upper Level

Cyprian Ekwensi: *For a Roll of Parchment*
William Conton: *The Flights*
Patrick Fagbola: *Kaduna Mafia*
Jeremiah Essien: *In The Shadow of Death*
Rose Njoku: *Withstand the Storm*
Okinba Launko: *Minted Coins* (Poetry)
Chinua Achebe: *Anthills of the Savannah*

Intermediate Level

Chinelo Achebe: *The Last Laugh & Other Stories*

Junior Level

A.O. Oyekanmi: *The Lion and the Hare*
Augustus Adebayo: *Once Upon a Village*

The Eye of the Earth

(Poems)

. . . temporary basement and
lasting roof breadbasket
and compost bed . . .
. . . .
Our earth will see again
this earth, OUR EARTH

The Eye of the Earth

(Poems)

Niyi Osundare

HEINEMANN EDUCATIONAL BOOKS (NIGERIA) Plc

Heinemann Educational Books (Nigeria) Plc
Head Office: 1 Ighodaro Road, Jericho, P.M.B. 5205, Ibadan
Phone: (02) 2412268, 2410943; Fax: (02) 2411089, 2413237.
E-mail: info@heinemannbooks.com

Area Offices and Branches
Abeokuta . Akure . Bauchi . Benin City . Calabar . Enugu . Ibadan
Ikeja . Ilorin . Jos . Kano . Katsina . Maiduguri . Makurdi . Minna
Owerri . Port Harcourt . Sokoto . Uyo . Yola . Zaria

© Niyi Osundare 1986
First published 1986
Reprinted 1988, 1996, 2000

ISBN 978 129 139 7

All Rights Reserved

No part of this publication may be reproduced, stored in a retrieval system or transmitted in any form or by any means, electronic, mechanical, photocopying, recording, or otherwise, without the prior permission of Heinemann Educational Books (Nigeria) Plc.

This book is sold subject to the condition that it should not by way of trade or otherwise be lent, re-sold, hired out or otherwise circulated without the publisher's prior consent in any form of binding or cover other than that in which It is published and without a similar condition including this condition being imposed on the subsequent purchaser.

Printed by Nazareth Press, Ibadan

Dedicated to
> **OUR EARTH**

and all who struggle to see it neither
> wastes
> > nor
> > > wants

Contents

	Pages
Preface	x
Earth	1

back to earth

Forest Echoes	3
The Rocks Rose to Meet Me	13
Harvestcall	18

eyeful glances
rainsongs

Let the Earth's Pain Be Soothed	27
First Rain	29
Rain-coming	30
Raindrum	32
Meet Me at Okeruku	33
Who Says that Drought Was Here?	34
But Sometimes When It Rains	36

homecall

Dawncall	39
Excursion	41
Farmer-born	43
They Too Are the Earth	45
What the Earth Said	46
Ours to Plough, Not to Plunder	48
Our Earth Will Not Die	50

PREFACE

Farmer-born, peasant-bred, I encountered dawn in the enchanted corridors of the forest, suckled on the delicate aroma of healing herbs, and the pearly drops of generous moons. Living in those early days was rugged, but barns brimmed with yams fattened by merciful rains and the tempering fire of the upland sun. The cock rang the bell of dawn, promptly aided by a lone and distant corn-mill which hummed into action, making sure it carried the village along. Earth was ours, and we earth's. We grew what we ate and ate what we grew. Famines there were, though few and far between, and in such leansome times, when yam was too distant to heed the summon of the stomach, we sacrificed grains to that demanding god.

Thus, then, was the story before the schoolyard jilted the farmstead and the bell emptied boisterous playing grounds into dreary classrooms where the teacher loomed like a forgiveless cane, sterner than a stone statue. Thus, then, the story before the virulent advent of Europe's merchants who turned native farmers into cocoa-coffee-cashew croppers, while yamfields succumbed to weeds and granaries rang out like mourning shells. A cancerous god called MONEY crashed in from across the seas, with a blind sword and a crown of noisy gold, smashing old customs, assailing the very core of ancient humanistic ethos. To acquire it on Europe's terms, Africa abandoned what she ate, committing her fertile soil and rugged energy to those alien crops which cushioned the European stomach. (Whoever still doesn't know the roots of Africa's hunger should run a rapid eye back to these uneasy epochs).

The poems in this collection are a journey into these times and beyond, when the earth's head stood on its neck and a hand sprouted but five fingers. If there is a passionate nostalgia in the rendering it is the legitimate flame of the inevitable fire often kindled when an embattled present makes a forward thrust difficult (surely not impossible!), and looking back becomes one of the weapons against a looming monster. But all this resides in the house of memory where doors open into the backyard of time, and windows bare their breasts for the knowing shafts of coming suns. For in the intricate dialectics of human living, looking back is looking forward; the visionary artist is not only a rememberer, he is also a reminder.

The 'Forest' in the first movement (the volume is conceived in three movements: 'back to earth', 'rainsongs', and 'homecall', with 'eyeful glances' functioning as their episodic diaphragm) is, essentially, shades and shadows of a remembered landscape, echoes of an Eden long departed when the rain forest was terrifyingly green though each tree, each vine, each herb, each beast, each insect, had its name in the baffling baptism of Nature.

Left mostly now are echoes whispered in the stubborn ears of memory. Most of those trees so vivaciously native to this forest have met a rapid death in the hands of timber merchants whose exploitative improvidence is symbolized here by the ubiquitous *agbègilòdó* (timber lorry). In a land where vision and humanistic sympathy have taken leave of the ruling class, hardly is there any policy aimed at stopping the parlous depletion of our natural being. Hardly is anyone aware that today's profit (for them) is tomorrow's irreparable loss for universal humanity.

'The Rocks Rose to Meet Me' is a homecoming of a kind, a journey back (and forth) into a receding past which still has a right to live. The rocks celebrated in this section, *Olosunta, Oroole* (both wonder siblings of Esidale), occupy a central place in the cosmic consciousness of Ikere people; they are worshipped and frequently appeased with rare gifts, thunderous drumming and dancing. But it must be stressed that these rocks are dramatized in this volume as a *creative, material essence,* as lasting monuments of time and place. Indeed, in addition to the mystic dimension, Ikere people also perceive the rocks as guardians of the harvest spirit, a feeling which informs the stem and stalk of 'Harvestcall', the final beat of the first movement.

In a way, 'rainsongs' is a logical continuation of 'forest echoes', it being a celebration of the giver and sustainer of life. As agent of the difference between plenty and famine, life and death, the rain occupied a godlike place in the consciousness of Ikere's agrarian people.

'Homecall', the final movement, raises vital queries, amplifies crucial fears about the state of earth, our home. With nuclear dust in the hearth and acid rain on the roof, just how will tomorrow's children live? The vision which provokes this question is, in the main, not very distant from that which has fired The Green Peace, The Women of Greenham Common, Operation Stop the Desert, The Save the Amazon Committee, and the millions of *human* beings who frequently troop out in European and American cities, urging that we give the human race priority over the arms race.

Waters are dying, forests are falling. A desert epidemic stalks a world where the rich and ruthless squander earth's wealth on the invention of increasingly accomplished weapons of death, while millions of people perish daily from avoidable hunger.

Tomorrow bids us tread softly, wisely, justly, lest we trample the eye of the EARTH.

Niyi Osundare

Ibadan
November 1985

Earth

Temporary basement
and lasting roof

first clayey coyness
and last alluvial joy

breadbasket
and compost bed

rocks and rivers
muds and mountains

silence of the twilight sea
echoes of the noonsome tide

milk of mellowing moon
fire of tropical hearth

spouse of the roving sky
virgin of a thousand offsprings

Ọgẹ́ẹ́rẹ́ amọ́kọ́yẹrí *

*The one that shaves his head with the hoe.

back to earth

Forest Echoes

(*with flute & heavy drums*)

A green desire, perfumed memories,
a leafy longing lure my wanderer feet
to this forest of a thousand wonders.
A green desire for this petalled umbrella
of simple stars and compound suns.
Suddenly, so soberly suddenly,
the sky is tree-high
and the horizon dips into an inky grove
like a masquerade scribbling loric fear
in the lines of festival streets.

        The rains have kept their time this year
        (Earth has (finally) won the love of the sky)
        Trees bob with barkward sap
        and leaves grab a deepening green
        from the scanty sun.

Bouncing boughs interlock overhead
like wristwrestlers straining muscularly
on a canvas of leaves wounded
by the fists of time
I tread, soft-soled, the compost carpet
of darkling jungles
my nose one charmed universe
of budding herbs and ripening roots

I tread the compost carpet of darkling forests
where terror grows on trembling leaves
natured by lore
nurtured by fairy truths

Here, under this awning, ageless,
the clock, unhanded, falls
in the deep belly of woods
its memory ticking songfully
in *elulu's** sleepless throat
Mauled the minutes, harried the hours;
taunted is time whose needle's eye
gates our comings and goings
time which wombed the moon
to bear the sun,
the hole in the ragged wardrobe
the gap in the ageing teeth
the bud on the ripening tree
Oh time,
coffin behind the cot.

And every toemark on the footpath
every fingerprint on every bark
the ropy climbers flung breathlessly
from tree to tree
the haunting sound and silence
of this sweet and sour forest
dig deep channels to the sea of memory.
And the outcome:
      will it be flow or flood . . .

    * * * * * *

> This is Oke Ubo Abusoro,
> the distant forest which shames the lazy leg,
> where the *oro* tree hawks lofty fruit
> for the blue children of a hungry sky
> where pampered yams break heaps' bounds
> and the plaintain leans earthwards
> with the joy of heavy harvest.
> This is Ubo Abusoro
> where my first faltering steps
> broke the earthworm on the path of dawn

Here still they are
those midgets which mirrored monsters
in our green eyes
Here they are
midget and monster still,
their unlikenesses now expanding
in the pupil of our schooling eyes.
A forest of a million trees, this,
a forest of milling trees
wounded, though, by time's axe
and the greedy edges of *agbegilodo's*** matchet
A stump here, a stump there
like a finger missing from a crowded hand
swarmed by struggling shoots,
unapparent heirs to fallen heights.

Iroko wears the crown of the forest,
town's rafter, roof of the forest
ironwood against the termites of time
Iroko wears the crown of the forest
its baobab foot rooted against
a thousand storms.

Iroko wears the crown of the forest,
Scourge of the sweating sawyer
the champion machet assays a bite,
beating a blunted retreat to the whetting stone.
The ironwood wears the crown of the forest.

Incapable of the hardy majesty of iroko,
Oganwo wears the surrogate crown
of heights and depths;
wounded by wanton matchets,
bled by the curing cutlass of the *babalawo*
the homing sun closes your weeping wounds
even as your doctor juice simmers
in the potions at dusk.

They take solace in *ayunre's* laughing stem
matchets sent sheathwards
by *iroko's* haughty hardness
Oh *ayunre!*
feather tree of the forest
willing wick of the blazing hearth,
the soft mouth which shouts an easy yes
to the asking cutlass.

Let iroko wear the crown of the roof
let ayunre play the clown of the fireplace,
but let no tree challenge the palm,
evergreen conqueror of rainless seasons.
Let no tree challenge the palm
mother of nuts and kernels
tree proud and precious like the sculptor's wood
bearer of wine and life:

short plump palmlets which pamper
the belly of unventuring gourds,
their unreachable parents
like some faraway land
now too tall, too thin, too distant
for the climbing rope
let no tree mock their aged brows
pockmarked with the blind bullets
of wasteful wars.

Their scaly stems, their thinning necks,
their faltering foliage swaying noise
lessly in the sleepless mirror of Ogbese,
Osun's rebel daughter (mother and child
parted somewhere below the mountains
pursuing a truce towards the settling sea);
her luggage of sand and rock
slicing the hills like a liquid knife,
parting the raceful turf between
the legs of trees
tunnelling through coy caves
descending on lowing rocks
with the youthsome clatter
of capering cascades
spanning bridges of fallen mahogany
throbbing with fishlets and tadpoles,
temporary semicolons hastening to
the unpunctuated period of the looming sea.

A bevy of birds, a barrack of beasts,
a school of truant antelopes
obey my headmasterly steps.

The partridge, alert like roadside grass,
roars in the clearing
its skyful guffaw a triumphant mockery
of a missing shot;
the hunter watches in flightless ire
his powder doused by drops
of salivating anger.

The weaverbird hears the laughter,
its nest swinging timelessly
in the trilling wind,
singing mute straws into eloquent patterns.
The forest throbs with the ceaseless chattering
of busy beaks.

Palm-bound, scalpel-toothed,
the squirrel pierces the tasty iris
of stubborn nuts;
adzeman of the forest,
those who marvel   the canine fire
in your mouth,
let them seek refuge in the fluffy grace
of your restless tail.

Let them, just like this chamelion
which dazzles the forest
with a garment of a million mirrors:

>   Count your colours, oh chamelion,
>   aborigine of wood and wind
>   count your colours

in the rainbow of the fern,
in the thick, ashen hide
of the sappling tree.
Count your colours,
oh prince of easy wardrobe,
dandy hueman who walks
so natively naked because he has
a forest of a thousand garbs.

Don the earth
with the preening prudence
of your global eyes.
Don the earth,
not with the millenial leaplessness
of millipede legs
not with the ireful fire
of the scorpion's tail
nor the calculating meanness
of the snail who carries his home
on every journey.

Don this praying mantis
in its eternal tabernacle
wringing green hands before
an absent god
Don the unlistening forest
salaaming (instead) to the
compelling muezzin of a loud,
insistent wind.
Don this praying brood,
this school of dancing twigs
Don this brood, praying,

like a flock of green *aladura*
in their noise-and-sand retreat.
Behold, too, these preyers
in the cannibal calvary
of the forest:
the *iroko* which swallows the shrub,
the hyena which harries the hare,
the elephant which tramples the grass
its legs nerveless with the gangrene
of senseless power
Tell them all the calm behind the claw
Tell them the sun
which succeeds the night.

*

My parting eyes arrest the anthill,
pyramid of the forest,
with a queenly Pharaoh swollen
with stony orders,
block-headed termites building
moatless castles, brittle turrets
ceaselessly wounded by the arrows
of the rain;
laying bricks and eggs
their milling chambers tenanted
by lashes of unquestioning labour
laying bricks and eggs
their winged tribe akimbo
standing in some safe and sweatless shade;
and when houndling hoofs assail the castle,
they seek ready sanctuary

in the castle of their wings.
Laying bricks and eggs

and when these eggs are hatched
will they, too, adult into
a brick-laying brood,
unquestioning?

My parting eyes sing silent requiems
to the vertebra of expired snakes
lying unstately on the roadside turf;
the same which only last season
eased off its hide
in the sumptuous wardrobe
of fallen foliage
like a striptease gleaming
before a colony of clapping ferns.

My parting eyes wave beckoning hands
to *patonmo*,***
coy mistress of gallant pilgrims,
swooning, swooning at every touch.
Old men say your corset is calico
your underskirt of fastest steel.
But after each protest, your leafy guards
are down again
down, when the invading stallions are gone
when their restless hoofs
have hit the flying dust.
Up, again, your eyelids
winged like an unuttered summon.
Coy mistress,

back again your veins and veils.

I can hear their chorus of parting songs:
the monkey which jolts the gym of towering boughs,
the gazelle which graces the grass
with maidensome glamour
the snake which echoes the rustle
of my parting feet.

And now
Memory,
loud whisper of yester-voices
confluence of unbroken rivers,
lower your horse of remembrance

Let me dismount.

   * a kind of bird which hoots at regular hours of the day
  ** timber lorry
*** a plant with small leaves which 'fold up' when touched;
    also called 'touch-me-not'.

The rocks rose to meet me

1

(To be chanted with agba drum throbbing in the background)

The rocks rose to meet me
like passionate lovers on a long-awaited tryst.
The rocks rose to meet me
their peaks cradled in ageless mists.
Olosunta* spoke first
the eloquent one
whose mouth is the talking house of ivory
Olosunta spoke first
the lofty one whose eyes are
balls of the winking sun
Olosunta spoke first
the riddling one whose belly is wrestling ground
for god and gold.

"You have been long, very long, and far',
said he, his tongue one flaming flash
of unburnable gnomes
"Unwearying wayfarer,
your feet wear the mud of distant waters
your hems gather the bur
of fartherest forests;
I cán see the westmost sun
in the mirror of your wandering eyes".

So saying, he smiled

the trees swaying their leafy heads
in the choreography of his moving lips
so saying, the sun lifted the wrinkle of clouds
from the face of a frowning sky.

Olosunta spoke first
the elephant hand which hits the haughty man in the head
and his testicles leak to the wondering earth
like overripe *oro* fruits in a thunderstorm
Olosunta spoke
his belly still battle ground of god and gold.
The god I have killed
since wisdom's straïghtening sun
licked clean the infant dew of fancy
The gold let us dig,
not for the gilded craniums
of hollow chieftains
(time's undying sword awaits their necks
who deem this earth their sprawling throne).
With the gold let us turn hovels into havens
paupers into people (not princes)
so hamlets may hear
the tidings of towns
so the world may sprout a hand
of equal fingers.

Yield your gold, lofty one.
But how dig the gold
without breaking the rock?

II

Oroole** came next
his ancient voice tremulous
in the morning air
(harmattans here whip with the flaying fury
of a slavemaster,
but how can we banish them
without a season of unripened peas?)

Pyramid of the brood,
you who rob your head to pay your foot:
for earth is where we stand
earth is where we strive,
and what greater vantage to a wrestling rock
than a platform of a thousand feet?

Behold, cornfields flourish around your foot
elephant grass fallows the land
for unborn harvests.
Swell the grain
with living water from your rocky arteries,
fatten the tuber,
so the hoe does not scoop a sterile clod
so the dibble does not drill a defeaned dross.
Pyramid of the brood
whose unclosing eyes witness
every stoke and every dot at *Amoye*.***·
You who loomed so fearsomely close
in the harmattan dawns of our learning days
before withdrawing into stony distance
with the noonward sun.

III

The rocks rose to meet me
Tall rocks, short rocks
sharp rocks, round rocks:
some with the staid steps
of war-wise warriors
others with the gaysome gaits
of pandering pilgrims.

The rocks rose to meet me
eloquent in their deafening silence.
The rocks rose
their shadows a robe
of ungatherable hems

IV
(The drums quieting)

I saw the invisible toe-marks
of Esidale
indelible on the spine-less column
of rocks
unrubbable like a birthmark
older than God
hieroglyphed when earth was molten pap
sculpted into stone by the busy hands
of wind and water.

I saw toe-marks
which laked the rain
for the waiting sun
thirsty like a Sahara camel

I read the cipher tattooed
on the biceps of stone
open like a book of oracles.

The rocks rose to meet me,
their legs lithesome sith lithic lore.
At every step the earth shook
like an ancient deck
trees trembled from roof to root.
The rocks rose to meet me
with ankle-bells of 'ploding pods
and seeds scattered like a million beads.
The rocks rose to meet my wanderer eyes
singing songs of sunken suns and worsted winds.

      with such defiant brows
      with such unfurrowed faces

just what have the rains been doing?

---

* a huge, imposing rock in **Ikere**, worshipped yearly during the popular **Olosun-ta festival**; reputed to be a repository of gold.

** a pyramid-shaped rock, also in **Ikere**.

*** Amoye Grammar School - sited under the shadows of **Oroole**.

Harvestcall

(*To be chanted to lively* **bata** *music*)

I

This is Iyanfoworogi
where, garnished in green
pounded yam rested its feted arms
on the back of stooping stakes.
This is Iyanfoworogi
where valiant heaps cracked, finally,
from the unquenchable zeal of fattening yams.

This is Iyanfoworogi
where yams, ripe and randy,
waged a noisy war against the knife;
here where, subbued by fire,
efuru* provoked mouthful clamour
from the combat of hungry wood:
      the pestle fights the mortar
      the mortar fights the pestle
      a dough of contention smooths down
      the rugged anger of hunger.

Here where yam wore the crown
in the reign of swollen roots
amid a retinue of vines and royal leaves;
between insistent sky and yielding earth,
the sun mellowed planting pageants
into harvest march,
a fiery pestle in his ripening hand.

this is Iyanfoworogi
where a tempting yam sauntered
out of the selling tray
and the marketplace became a mob
of instant suitors.

II

And this Oke Eniju
where coy cobs rocked lustily
in the loin of swaying stalks.
Once here in May
a tasselled joy robed the field
like hemless green.
Once here in May
the sky was a riot of pollen grains
and ivory mills waited (im)patiently
for the browning of grey tassels.

And when June had finally grabbed the year
by her narrow waist
corn cobs flashed their milky teeth
in disrobing kitchens.
Plenty's season announced its coming
and the humming mill at dawn
suddenly became the village heart.

III

(Finally) Ogbese Odo
where cotton pods, lips duly parted
by December's sun,

draped busy farmsteads
in a harvest of smiles.
Here a blooming loom curtailed
the tiger claws of the harmattan
and earth's wardrobe lent a garb
to every season.

IV

(*Music lowers in tempo, becoming solemn*)

But where **are** they?
Where are they gone:
aroso, geregede, otiili, pakala**
which beckoned lustily to the reaping basket
Where are they
the yam pyramids which challenged the sun
in busy barns
Where are they
the pumpkins which caressed earthbreast
like mammary burdens
Where are they
the pods which sweetened harvest air
with the clatter of dispersing seeds?
Where are they? Where are they gone?

Uncountable seeds lie sleeping
in the womb of earth
uncountable seeds
awaiting the quickening tap
of our waking finger.

With our earth so warm
How can our hearth be so cold?

---

* the king of yams
** all four are types of beans.

eyeful glances

The desert caller
comes on a camel
of clouds,
undulates through the dunes
of hazy shadows
        &
gliding through the open welcome
of January's door
whispers urgent tidings
in the ears of my skin

    * * * * * *

a few teasing drops
on earth's gaping lips
vanishing like droplets
on a steel plate
hot with the forge's red rage

    * * * * * *

a tree leaflets the sprawling lawn
the grass reads between the veins
and up they rise
against trampling feet
borrowing anthems from the whistling wind.

    * * * * * *

a timid rain peeps behind the clouds
then recoils
abandoning the world

to the gruelling heat
of a hungry season

* * * * * *

a parting cloud
grips the trigger
of a homing day
the sun bursts out
in a staccato
of orange idioms

* * * * * *

the flame tree
coifs the forest
in petals of fire
(it's the tinder season)
awaiting the waters of March

* * * * * *

the evening sky spreads out
like a mat
for a sun about to sleep
distant trees wave orange hands
to a homing prince.

* * * * * *

broadfaced like a Kabuki mask
the westering sun

dips a bloodshot eye
in the eloquent eye
of an evening lake

* * * * * *

a desperate match
stabs the night
in the gloomy alleys
of *NEPA's** darkdom
the distance glows
with sparks of amber blood.

a careless match, a harmattan rage
our farms are tinder
for a dispossessing flame;
a criminal torch, an incendiary plot
a blaze conceals the trails
of looters of state.

*National Electric Power Authority

rainsongs

Let Earth's Pain Be Soothed

(for the one who brought rainy news from Under-the-Rock)
(to the accompaniment of a flute and/or the rain drum)

The sky carries a boil of anguish
Let it burst

Our earth has never lingered so dry
in the season of falling showers
clouds journey over trees and over hills
miserly with their liquid treasure

The sky carries a boil of anguish
Let it burst

Prostrate like famished horses
brown hills cast vacant looks
at balded plains where playing kids
provoke the dust in what once was
the cradle of green

The sky carries a boil of anguish
Let it burst

Dust
dust in brewing kitchens

dust in eating halls
dust in busy bedrooms
dust in scheming boardrooms
dust in retrenching factories
dust in power brothels

The sky carries a boil of anguish
Let is burst

Let it rain today
   that parched throats may sing
Let it rain
   that earth may heal her silence
Let it rain today
   that cornleaves may clothe the hills
Let it rain
   that roots may swell the womb of lying plains
Let it rain today
   that stomachs may shun the rumble of thunder
Let it rain
   that children may bath and bawl and brawl

The sky carries a boil of anguish
Let it burst

The roofs have been silent too long
the seeds noiseless in the dormitory of the soil
the earth has been lying too long, and songless.

Time to leap, time to lilt

Let the sky's boil of anguish burst today
The pain of earth be soothed.

First Rain

a tingling tang awakes the nose
when the first rain has just clipped
the wing of the haughty dust
a cooling warmth embraces
our searching soles
as the land vapour rises
like a bootless infantry

and
through her liberated pores
    our earth breathes again.

Rain-Coming

Slowly
    but
        surely
the early rains ring the bell
and the earth springs green
from the sleep of brown

slowly
    but
        surely
like liquid fingers
on the aluminium drum
of echoing roofs
the rain unties the farmer's tongue,
bursting famine yawns
into barns of lilting yams
plums and pumpkins
dense with drink and daring
roll juicily from furrow to furrow

slowly
    but
        surely
the elephant grass caresses wayfarers
with the tuskless blade
of savannah leaves
laughing partridges arouse the tender grass

grasscutters take cover for their tasty flesh

slowly
    but
        surely
the early rains ring the bell
but oh my land!
so deep and dry still
in the unnatural desert
of barn-burners.

Raindrum

The roofs sizzle at the waking touch,
talkative like kettledrums
tightened by the iron fingers of drought

Streets break into liquid dance
gathering legs in the orchestra of the road
Streets break into liquid dance
gliding eloquently down the apron of the sky

A stray drop saunters down the thatch
of my remembrance
waking memories long dormant
under the dry leaves of time:

>of caked riverbeds
>and browned pastures
>of baking noons
>and grilling nights
>of earless cornfields
>and tired tubers

Then
Lightning strikes its match of rain
Barefoot, we tread the throbbing earth,

Renewed

Meet me at Okeruku

Meet me at *Okeruku**
where earth is one compact
of reddening powder
daubed coquettishly
on the harmattan brow
of trembling houses

And when the rains are here
when this dust is clod and clay
show me your camwood shoes
show me hurried toemarks
on the ciphered pages of narrow alleys
awaiting the liquid erazer
of the next shower

---

* a red-earth district in Ikere.

Who says that drought was here?

With these green guests around
Who says that drought was here?

The rain has robed the earth
in vests of verdure
the rain has robed an earth
licked clean by the fiery tongue of drought

With these green guests around
Who says that drought was here?

Palms have shed the shroud of brown
cast over forest tops
by the careless match of tinder days
when flares flooded the earth
and hovering hawks taloned the tale
to the ears of the deafening sky

With these green guests around
Who says that drought was here?

Aflame with herbal joy
trees slap heaven's face
with the compound pride
of youthful leaves

drapering twigs into groves
once skeletal spires in
the unwinking face of the baking sun

With these green guests around
Who says that drought was here?

And anthills throw open their million gates
and winged termites swarm the warm welcome
of compassionate twilights
and butterflies court the fragrant company
of fledgeling flowers
and milling moths paste wet lips
on the translucent ears of listening windows
and the swallow brailles a tune
on the copper face of the gathering lake
and weaverbirds pick up the chorus
in the leafening heights . . .
soon crispy mushrooms will break
the fast of venturing soles

With these green guests around
Who still says that drought was here?

But sometimes when it rains

But sometimes when it rains
and an angry thunder raps earth's ears
with its hands of fire
Sometimes when it rains
and a heartless storm beheads
the poor man's house
like some long-convicted felon,

> Sometimes when it rains
> you wonder who sent the skies weeping

Sometimes when it rains
and an impregnable mahogany falls
across your farmward path
sometimes when it rains
and a streamlet swollen with watery pride
drowns your fields and tender tubers

> Sometimes when it rains
> you wonder who sent the skies weeping

Sometimes when it rains
and a diligent tryst is washed out
by a careless downpour
sometimes when it rains
and a callous mist thickens
between you and the waiting one
sometimes when it rains
dreams are wet with the desperate longing
of a jilted embrace

You wonder who sent the skies weeping sometimes when it rains.

homecall

Dawncall

Come with me at dawn
When a matchless darkness couples earth and sky
And the world is one starless bed of frigid sweat
Come with me
When trees listen earlessly to the accent
Of the waking wind
Head-deep in the indigo of night.

Mark, oh mark this misty mob breaking out
Of the mouth of a yawning world
Swaddling the glowworm's winking lamps
On the inky poles of a sleepless fog.
Mark the young moon managing a milky flight
From the trumpet ambush of the first cock

Eyelids laden with dew, the grass cannot see the lines on its palm; puking like a baby, darkling, earth cannot count the fingers on her drowsy hand. Wet and wild the earth, where is the sun? Wet and wild how count the hands of the dozing clock behind the back of its solar face? Wet and wild the clock dissolved in dew. Dissolved. Tickless like a heart, ethered. Earth is timeless. Time less. And a termless halo surrounds our head havened in the firmament of reigning mist. Oh! that mob from earth's yawning mouth. Wet and wild a prancing *eusa** scuttles across dawn's corridor, its jaws a silent mill of hoarded kernels. Wet and wild the toad, tail-less like a forgetting race, leapless like a senile mountain. Wet and wild like a wind unwitched. Solitary hour wet and wild, solitary like an only finger, wild like a virgin brush. Solitary this hour, the earth swarmed by minds and matters, monsters and manikins. Solitary. And soulitary? A deafening silence usurps the earth. Silence in the leaping lair. Silence. Silence in the munching mill. Silence. Silence in conquerred covens. Silence.

Mark this misty mob breaking out
Of the mouth of a yawning earth
And this earthworm
Whose blood will break the fast of earth
When this dawn is done.

---

* or **okete**, a nocturnal rodent.

Excursion

Past bush paths tarred by tireless treading
Past rocky outcrops rubbed smooth by stubborn heels
Past dandelions roaring silently at my wandering feet
Past elephant grass fluted tusklessly by the wind.

Past the depleted copper of harvested cornfields
Past the leafy grove of ripening yams
Past the groundnut's leguminous lilt
in the orchestra of swinging furrows
Past the bean which has a thousand kids
with antimony in each eye

Past the gallant butterfly dallying from flower to flower
Past the bee droning and dreaming in the hammock
of fallowing farms
Past the dung-beetle rolling in its forbidden ball
Past soldier ants bootless in their lengthy columns

Past the lake lying namelessly in the register
of famous shrubs
Past the duck which brailles liquid letters
on its open face
Past boulders and pebbles which answer the whisper
of calling feet
Past the quivering arrow of a noonward sun

Homeward

with a flower in one hand
Homeward
with a sun in the other
Homeward
To a house of sunful fragrance.

Farmer-Born

Farmer-born peasant-bred
I have frolicked from furrow to furrow
sounded kicking tubers in the womb
of quickening earth
and fondled the melon breasts
of succulent ridges.

Farmer-born peasant-bred
I have traced the earthworm's intricate paths
on the map of dawn
heeded dew-call to the upland farm
and, sun-sent, have sought *iroko* refuge
at hungry noons.

Farmer-born peasant-bred
I have lived on the aroma
of fresh-felled forests
relished the delicious symmetry
of *akee* apple colours
and plucked the pendulous promise of ripening
pawpaw

Farmer-born peasant-bred
I have rattled the fleshy umbrella
of mushroom jungles
rustled the compost carpet of fallen leaves
and savoured the songful clatter
of opening pods

Farmer-born peasand-bred
classroom-bled
I have thrown open my kitchen doors
and asked hunger to take a seat,
my stomach a howling dump
for Carolina rice.

They too are the earth

They too are the earth
the swansongs of beggars sprawled out
in brimming gutters
they are the earth
under snakeskin shoes and Mercedes tyres

> They too are the earth
> the sweat and grime of
> millions hewing wood and hurling water
> they are the earth
> muddy every pore like naked moles.

They too are the earth
the distant groans of thousands buried alive
in hard, unfathomable mines
They are the earth
of gold dreams and blood banks

> They too are the earth
> the old dying distant deaths
> in narrow abandoned hamlets
> they are the earth
> women battling centuries of
> *male*ficent slavery

Are they of this earth
who fritter the forest and harry the hills
Are they of this earth
who live that earth may die
Are they?

What The Earth Said

I have heard
>the thud of sleepy boots plodding
>toilwards in dreary dawns.

I have seen
>busy hands rouse a slumbrous yard
>into a hive of humming demons

I have shaken
>hands calloused by wood and steel

I have touched
>foreheads foraged by grit and grime

I have seen
>heavy rosters and light pockets

I have seen
>penuried lives, spent, in ghetto dungeons

I have seen
>foremen soulless like their whistling whips

I have seen
>native *executhieves* hold fort for alien wolves

I have seen
>labouring mouths famish like desert basins

I have seen
>factorylords roll in slothful excess

I have heard
>backs creak on heartless machines

I have felt
>lungs powdered with asbestos death

I have seen
      lives snuffed out like candles in the storm.

And the earth,
the earth receives these green fruits
with dusty tears,
the earth receives them
saying:
      behold these seeds planted so soon
      in the season before the rains
      let them sprout in the month
      of daring struggle;
      let them bloom
      and kill the killer pests.

Ours To Plough, Not To Plunder

The earth is ours to plough and plant
the hoe is her barber
the dibble her dimple

Out with mattocks and matchets
bring calabash trays and rocking baskets
let the sweat which swells earthroot
relieve heavy heaps of their tuberous burdens

Let wheatfields raise their breadsome hands
to the ripening sun
let legumes clothe the naked bosom
of shivering mounds
let the pawpaw swell and swing
its headward breasts

Let water spring
from earth's unfathomed fountain
let gold rush
from her deep unseeable mines
hitch up a ladder to the dodging sky
let's put a sun in every night

Our earth is an unopened grainhouse,
a bustling barn in some far, uncharted jungle
a distant gem in a rough unhappy dust

This earth is
>	ours to work not to waste
>	ours to man not to maim
This earth is ours to plough, not to plunder.

Our Earth Will Not Die
(*To a solemn, almost elegiac tune*)

    Lynched
        the lakes
    Slaughtered
        the seas
    Mauled
        the mountains

But our earth will not die

    Here
      there
        everywhere
a lake is killed by the arsenic urine
from the bladder of profit factories
a poisoned stream staggers down the hills
coughing chaos in the sickly sea
the wailing whale, belly up like a frying fish,
crests the chilling swansong of parting waters.

But our earth will not die.

    Who lynched the lakes. Who?
    Who slaughtered the seas. Who?
    Whoever mauled the mountains. Whoever?

Our earth will not die

And the rain
the rain falls, acid, on balding forests
their branches amputated by the septic daggers
of tainted clouds

Weeping willows drip mercury tears
in the eye of sobbing terrains
a nuclear sun rises like a funeral ball
reducing man and meadow to dust and dirt.

But our earth will not die.

Fishes have died in the waters.   Fishes.
Birds have died in the trees.   Birds.
Rabbits have died in their burrows.   Rabbits.

But our earth will not die

(Music turns festive, louder)

Our earth will see again
eyes washed by a new rain
the westering sun will rise again
resplendent like a new coin.
The wind. unwound, will play its tune
trees twittering, grasses dancing;
hillsides will rock with blooming harvests
the plains batting their eyes of grass and grace.
The sea will drink its heart's content
when a jubilant thunder flings open the skygate
and a new rain tumbles down
in drums of joy.
Our earth will see again

  this earth, OUR EARTH.

www.ingramcontent.com/pod-product-compliance
Lightning Source LLC
Chambersburg PA
CBHW060347250426
43669CB00056B/2544